VOCAL SELECTIONS

THE HUNCHBACK OF NOTRE DAME

ISBN 978-1-4950-9528-3

Walt Disney Music Company
Wonderland Music Company, Inc.

DISTRIBUTED BY

HAL•LEONARD®
7777 W. BLUEMOUND RD. P.O. BOX 13819 MILWAUKEE, WI 53213

In Australia Contact:
Hal Leonard Australia Pty. Ltd.
4 Lentara Court
Cheltenham, Victoria, 3192 Australia
Email: ausadmin@halleonard.com.au

Visit Hal Leonard Online at
www.halleonard.com

Professional and amateur theatrical licensing
available exclusively through

**MUSIC THEATRE
INTERNATIONAL**

Studio Cast Recording now available
on iTunes, Spotify, and Amazon Music

THE BELLS OF NOTRE DAME

Music by ALAN MENKEN
Lyrics by STEPHEN SCHWARTZ

OUT THERE

Music by ALAN MENKEN
Lyrics by STEPHEN SCHWARTZ

Flowingly, with building excitement

QUASIMODO:

Safe be-hind these win-dows and these par-a-pets of stone, gaz-ing at the peo-ple down be-low me. All my life I watch them as I hide up here a-lone, hun-gry for the his-to-ries they show me. All my life I mem-o-rize their

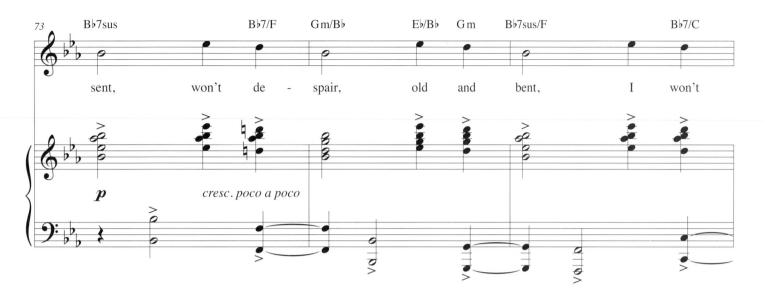

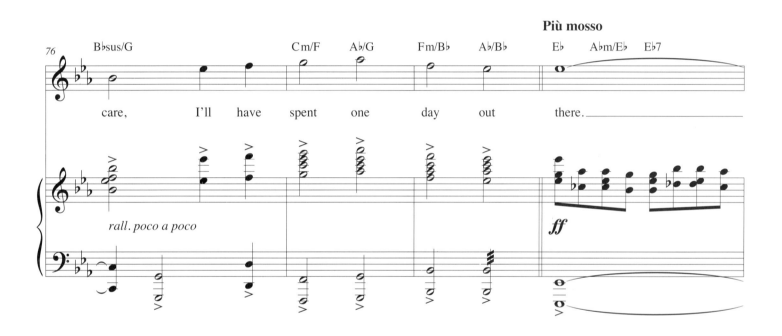

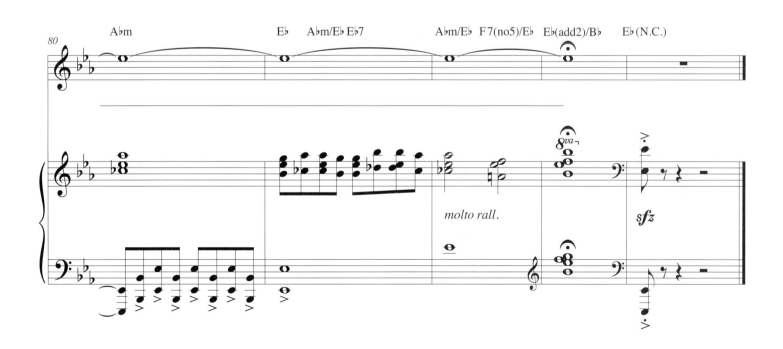

TOPSY TURVY

Music by ALAN MENKEN
Lyrics by STEPHEN SCHWARTZ

REST AND RECREATION

Music by ALAN MENKEN
Lyrics by STEPHEN SCHWARTZ

Like oth - er true knights, I've got am - bi - tion.

But for a few nights fun is my mis - sion. So, what do you say?

Care to share a day of rest and rec - re - a -

tion? _____

RHYTHM OF THE TAMBOURINE

Music by ALAN MENKEN
Lyrics by STEPHEN SCHWARTZ

GOD HELP THE OUTCASTS

Music by ALAN MENKEN
Lyrics by STEPHEN SCHWARTZ

TOP OF THE WORLD

Music by ALAN MENKEN
Lyrics by STEPHEN SCHWARTZ

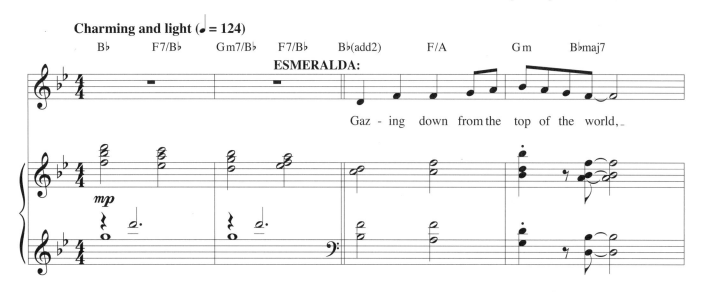

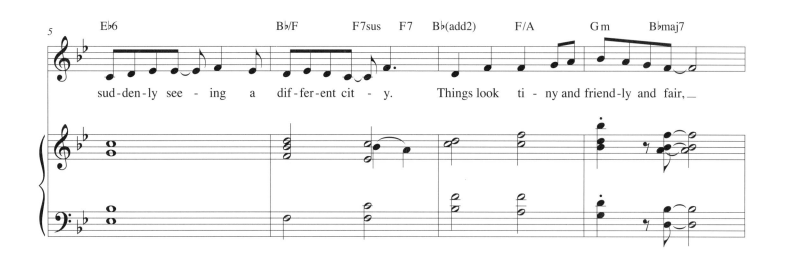

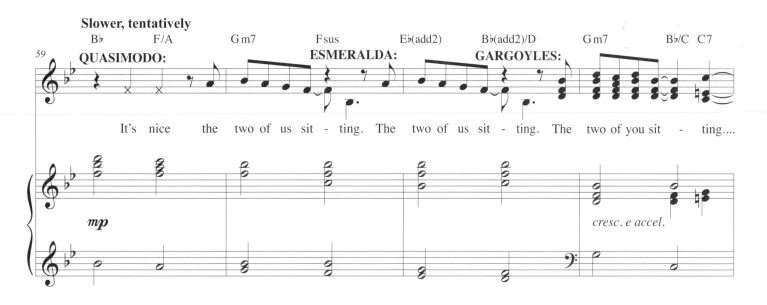

Slower, tentatively

QUASIMODO: It's nice the two of us sit - ting.

ESMERALDA: The two of us sit - ting.

GARGOYLES: The two of you sit - ting....

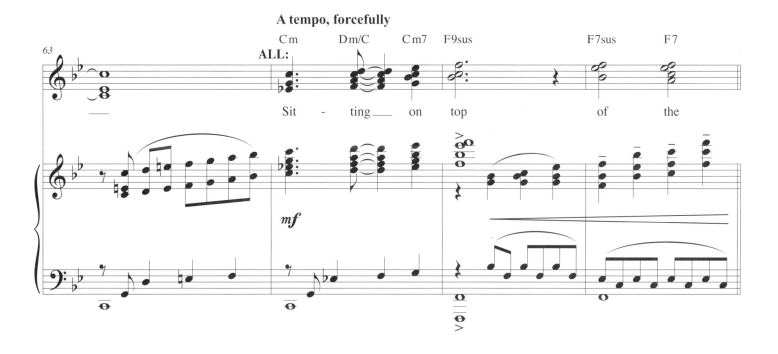

A tempo, forcefully

ALL: Sit - ting___ on top of the

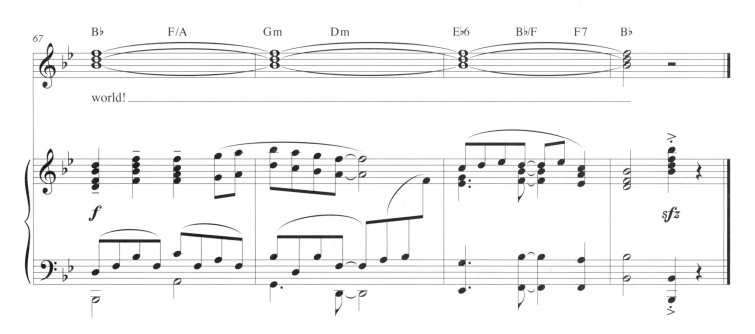

world!

TAVERN SONG
(Thai Mol Piyas)

Music by ALAN MENKEN
Lyrics by STEPHEN SCHWARTZ

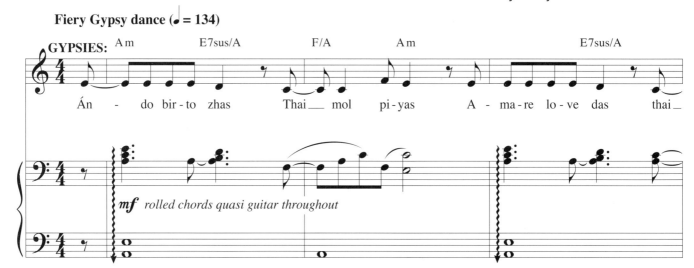

HEAVEN'S LIGHT

Music by ALAN MENKEN
Lyrics by STEPHEN SCHWARTZ

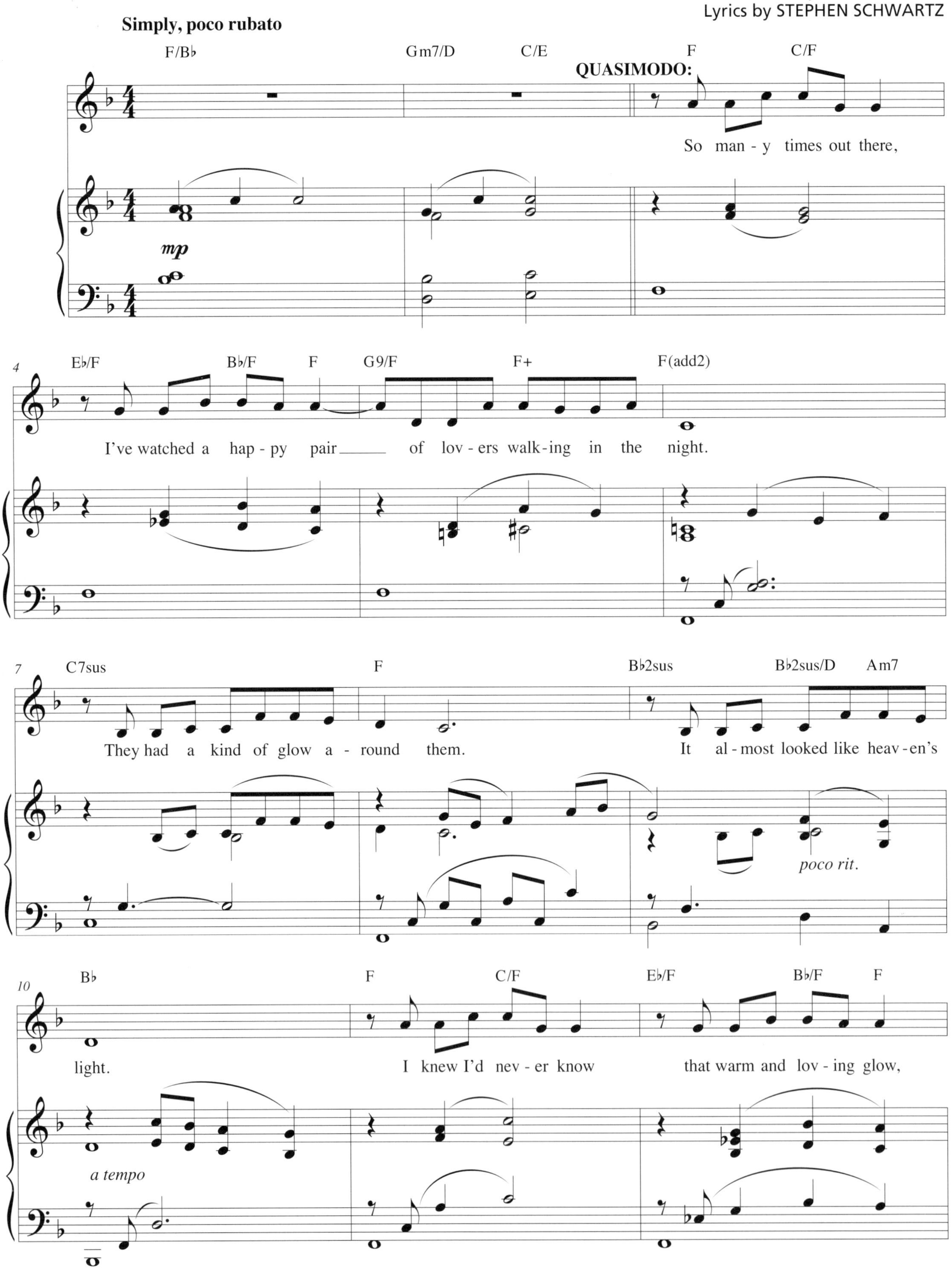

Simply, poco rubato
F/B♭ Gm7/D C/E F C/F
QUASIMODO:
So man - y times out there,
mp
E♭/F B♭/F F G9/F F+ F(add2)
I've watched a hap - py pair of lov - ers walk - ing in the night.
C7sus F B♭2sus B♭2sus/D Am7
They had a kind of glow a - round them. It al - most looked like heav - en's
poco rit.
B♭ F C/F E♭/F B♭/F F
light. I knew I'd nev - er know that warm and lov - ing glow,
a tempo

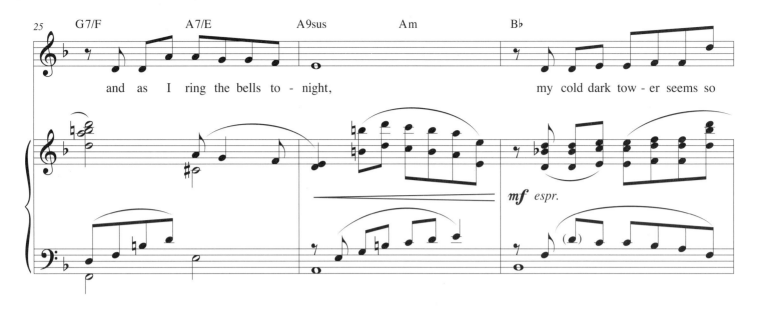

and as I ring the bells to - night, my cold dark tow - er seems so

Strict, moderate 4

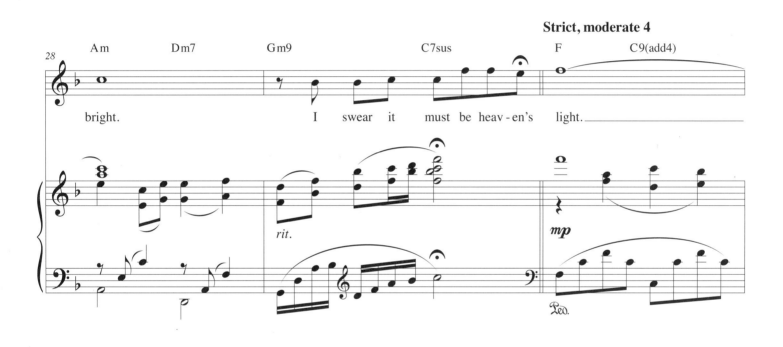

bright. I swear it must be heav - en's light.

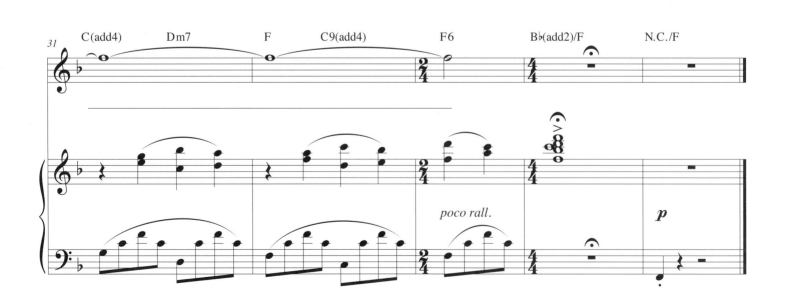

HELLFIRE

Music by ALAN MENKEN
Lyrics by STEPHEN SCHWARTZ

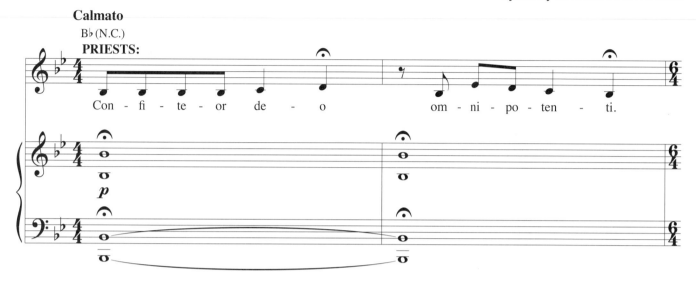

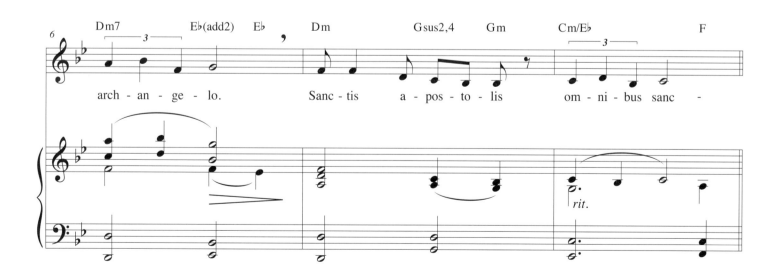

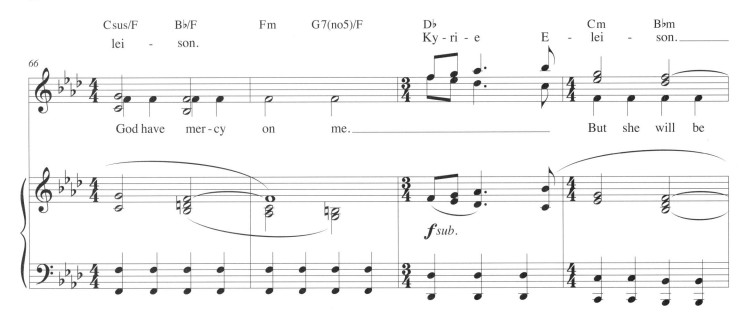

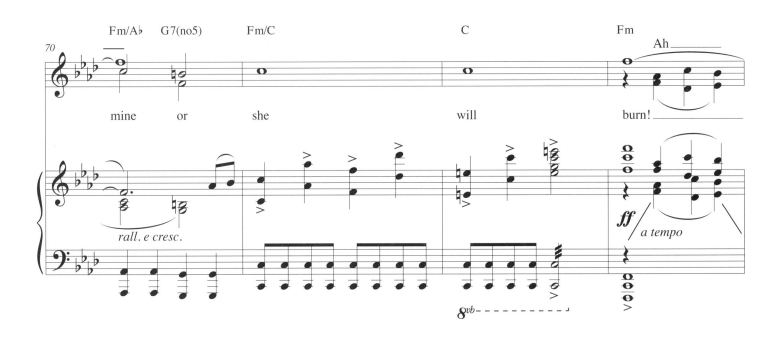

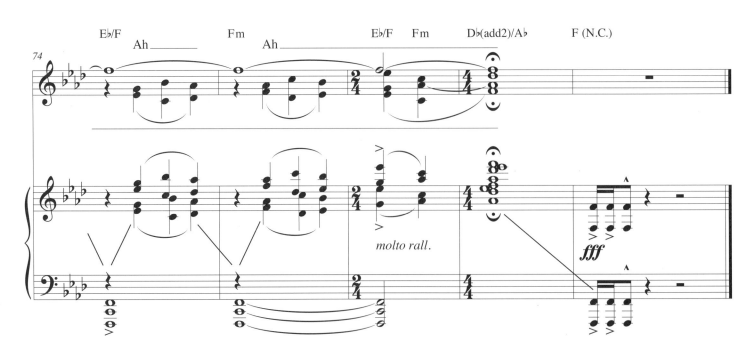

ESMERALDA

Music by ALAN MENKEN
Lyrics by STEPHEN SCHWARTZ

Moderately fast, with vigor

FROLLO:
Hunt down the gyp-sy Es-mer-al-da! Don't let her flee and van-ish in the night. These are the flames of Es-mer-al-da. While she is free, your torch-es must burn bright.

FLIGHT INTO EGYPT

Music by ALAN MENKEN
Lyrics by STEPHEN SCHWARTZ

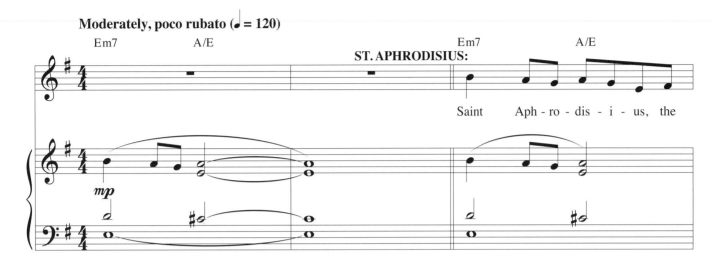

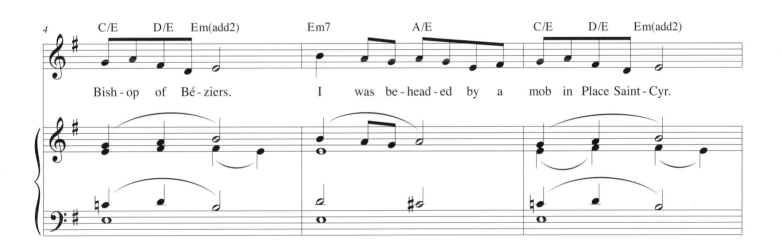

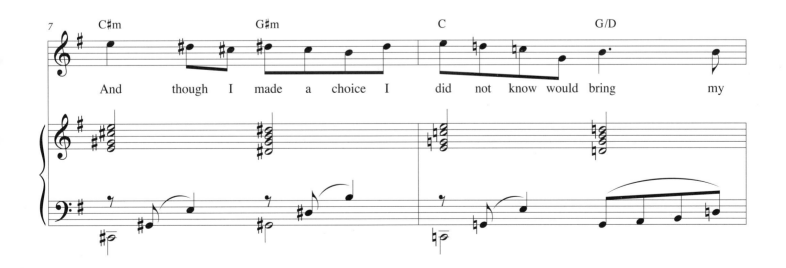

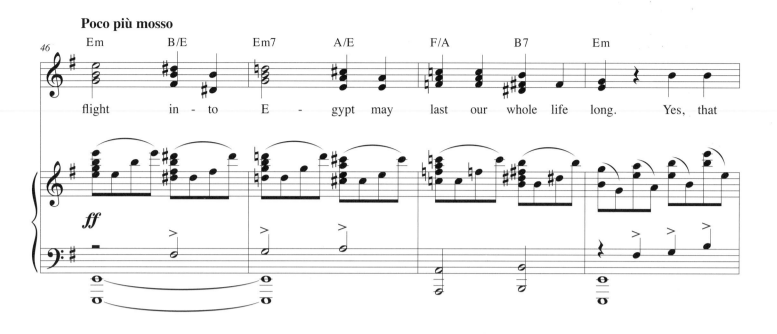

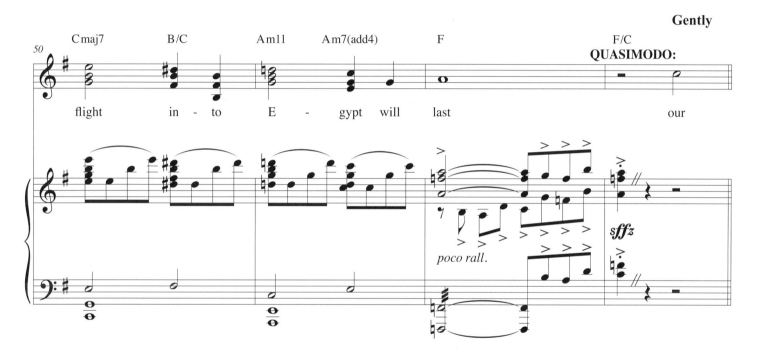

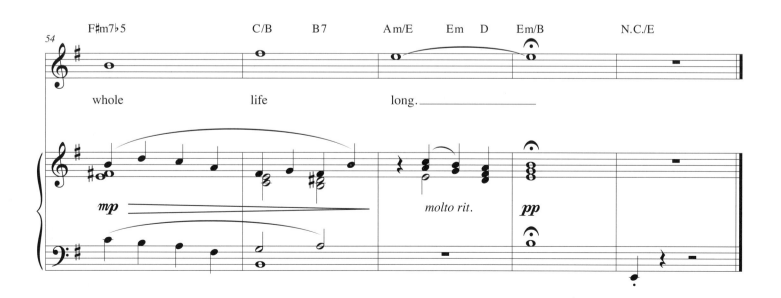

THE COURT OF MIRACLES

Music by ALAN MENKEN
Lyrics by STEPHEN SCHWARTZ

CLOPIN: May-be you've heard of a ter-ri-ble place where the scoun-drels of Pa-ris col-lect in a lair... May-be you've heard of that myth-i-cal place called the Court ___ of Mir-a-cles? ___ The Court ___ of Mir-a-cles!

IN A PLACE OF MIRACLES

Music by ALAN MENKEN
Lyrics by STEPHEN SCHWARTZ

SOMEDAY

Music by ALAN MENKEN
Lyrics by STEPHEN SCHWARTZ

MADE OF STONE

Music by ALAN MENKEN
Lyrics by STEPHEN SCHWARTZ

Seething, with power and anger (♩ = 90)

FINALE ULTIMO

Music by ALAN MENKEN
Lyrics by STEPHEN SCHWARTZ

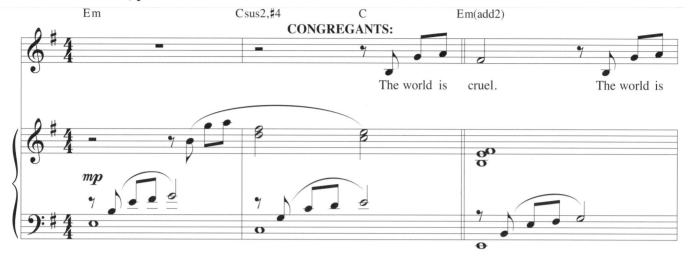

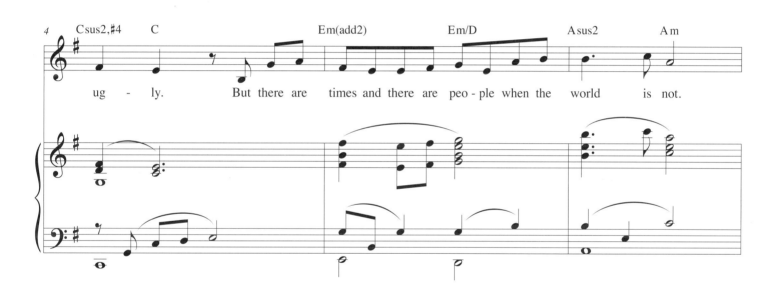

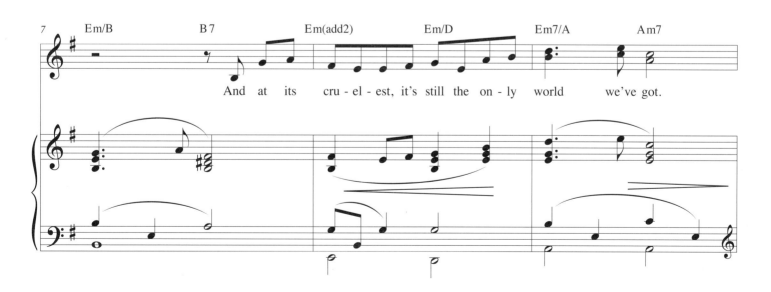